I0888958

THE MIDLAND REGION IN THE 1970s AND 1980s

Andy Gibbs

AMBERLEY

Front cover above: Resplendent in the sunshine is No. 86408 *St Johns Ambulance* working 1090, the 10.40 SO Edinburgh Waverley to Eastbourne. September 1989.

Front cover below: Chirping away at Ilkeston are Nos 20143 and 20197, seen working a train of loaded 16-ton coal wagons. August 1978. (A. Gibbs)

Back cover: Powering south at Ratcliffe-on-Soar with a Sheffield to St Pancras service is this unidentified split-headcode Class 45. Ratcliffe Power Station is to the right and an MGR train can be glimpsed. This is now the site of the East Midlands Parkway station. 1976.

First published 2019

Amberley Publishing
The Hill, Stroud
Gloucestershire, GL5 4EP

www.amberley-books.com

Copyright © Andy Gibbs, 2019

The right of Andy Gibbs to be identified as the Author of this work has been asserted in accordance with the Copyrights, Designs and Patents Act 1988.

ISBN 978 1 4456 8187 0 (print)
ISBN 978 1 4456 8188 7 (ebook)

All rights reserved. No part of this book may be reprinted or reproduced or utilised in any form or by any electronic, mechanical or other means, now known or hereafter invented, including photocopying and recording, or in any information storage or retrieval system, without the permission in writing from the Publishers.

British Library Cataloguing in Publication Data.
A catalogue record for this book is available from the British Library.

Typesetting by Aura Technology and Software Services, India. Printed in the UK.

Introduction

Welcome to the fourth of my regional photo albums. This is a fond look back at the Midland Region through the 1970s and '80s, when loose-coupled freights still lingered on, Peaks ruled the roost on cross-country services and West Coast services could be compared to a Simple Minds song – 81, 82, 83, 84 (you might need to look that up!). I hope you enjoy it.

The Midland Region to me was always about the long, slow, rattling unfitted freights, merry-go-round coal trains and colourful Freightliner services. Add to this the classes of diesel and electric locomotives that we were never likely to see south of London and you can see the fascination.

Day trips to London from my home in Brighton usually meant a few hikes up and down the Euston Road, bringing Euston, St Pancras and of course King's Cross into the mix.

I have relatives in Nottingham and at least twice a year we would venture north. Trips to Clay Cross, Toton or Trent Junction with my late Uncle Tony were always something to look forward to – although I'm not sure my long-suffering sister or cousins would agree!

Later trips by myself to Nottingham meant that St Pancras has always been a special place for me, with the two-hour journey on a fast train behind a lumbering Peak taking you past Cricklewood, Wellingborough, Leicester and Trent Junction to name but a few locations.

When staying at my relatives there was always a day or two out watching the trains, often at Nottingham or Derby station, with its mix of Midland Main Line and NE–SW services plus a never-ending stream of freight. My Student Railcard took me further afield to exotic locations such as Birmingham New Street, Guide Bridge or Crewe. The Manchester Piccadilly to Harwich train was a regular ride home to Nottingham as it reached there in time for a quick dash to the Broadmarsh bus station to catch the bus home in time for dinner!

Trips out from Nottingham by car took me to places such as Duffield, Ilkeston, Burton-on-Trent and Clay Cross. I think Clay Cross was without doubt my favourite location.

After my A Levels, a holiday in North Wales gave me plenty of trips to Chester and Crewe. All this time meant eking out a couple of 36 Exposure colour slide films and hoping there weren't too many duff ones.

Not ignoring the West Coast Main Line, trips included journeys to Rugby and Birmingham. Once I started work for British Rail the trips could be extended on my free passes. Falmer to Thurso on a ticket gave you plenty of route options through the Midlands!

This book will start off at Marylebone before heading north to Leamington Spa and coming back to London for the West London line and Kensington Olympia. This is followed by the West Coast Main Line out of Euston before we hit the Midland Main Line, as well as the Trans-Pennine and Settle & Carlisle routes. Pictures are mainly from 35 mm slides plus Medium Format slides and Medium Format black and white negatives.

Thank you once again to the numerous railway websites that are a labour of love 'keeping the gen alive' along with various Working Timetables and the 1Hxx series of books used in the research. Thank you also to my late Uncle Tony (credited as J. A. Lower), whose photos adorn these pages, and to the other photographers without whom this book would not exist.

Andy Gibbs
January 2019

We start our journey at Marylebone, which during the 1970s and '80s was a very run-down location. ADB968000 (formally BTH-built Class 15 D8243) is a train heating unit, converted back in 1969 after spending just under eight years in traffic. 12 April 1986.

Nos 25141 and 25129 wait to depart Marylebone with 1Z80, the Worcester Locomotive Society's 'Pennine Rose' railtour. These locos worked to New Street before being replaced by a pair of Class 20s. Full details can be found on www.sixbellsjunction.co.uk. 5 May 1979.

A mixed bag of wagons form the train behind No. 47076 *City of Truro* as it trundles through Aylesbury station. December 1982.

At Aylesbury we find 6B Hastings unit No. 1032 working the 'Hastings DEMU Farewell' railtour. These versatile units were a godsend to the Southern Region, being able to work anywhere. This railtour started at Hastings and covered the West London line, Watford, Stanmore, Marylebone, Reading and much more. 11 May 1986.

At Aynho Junction the route from Marylebone joins the line from Oxford through to the Midlands. Here we find No. 47561 framed by the signals with an unidentified cross-country service. 24 July 1986. (M. Hull)

No. 47451 in large logo livery heads south with an unidentified cross-country service at Aynho Junction. 27 May 1987. (M. Hull)

At Banbury Lane, King's Sutton, No. 47480 *Robin Hood* heads south in the afternoon with a service for the south coast. A later photo in the book shows No. 47480 shortly after it was named. 13 May 1982. (M. Hull)

Scurrying through King's Sutton station is a pristine-looking No. 47488 with an unidentified cross-country service. 6 May 1988. (M. Hull)

Banbury station is looking very tidy as No. 47509 *Albion* comes to a stand while working 1M50, the 09.20 Brighton to Manchester Piccadilly service. 15 April 1983. (J. Binnie)

Looking a bit rough around the edges, 'Hoover' No. 50038 *Formidable* waits to depart Banbury with 1V15, the 08.20 Liverpool Lime Street to Paddington. 30 August 1983. (G. Edwards)

With the driver photobombing the shot, No. 47803 is at Banbury with 1066, the 07.18 Manchester Piccadilly to Brighton service. 31 May 1989. (R. J. Williamson)

Just north of Banbury at Cropredy, famous for its music festival, No. 47575 *City of Hereford* slogs south with 1090, the 1050 Glasgow Central/Edinburgh to Brighton service. The 'Sussex Scot' seems to be overprovided for in the catering department with both an RBR and a Micro-Buffet in the formation. 7 September 1988. (M. Hull)

At Harbury we find 'Rat' No. 25263 with a short engineers' train. The loco still has the recess for the removed tablet catcher below the rear cab sidelight. 25 June 1976.

Unusual motive power, probably due to the weather. Here we find Nos 31231 and 31186 double-heading 1V28, the 10.25 Birmingham New Street to Paddington train. The combination is seen approaching Leamington Spa. 29 December 1976.

No. 25300 is berthed at Leamington Spa with a short train of open wagons. 12 August 1976.

In blizzard conditions an unidentified Class 47 is captured in the snow at Leamington Spa while working 1M12, the 11.05 Paddington to Birmingham New Street. The driver vainly looks back for the tip to depart. 13 January 1977.

At Leamington Spa a motley collection of DMUs form the 12.10 service for Birmingham Moor Street. From front to back is Gloucester Class 100 vehicle M50342, Class 108 vehicle M56267 and Cravens Class 105 car M50812. On the stops is Gloucester Class 122 M55006. 28 April 1978.

As staff load the train with mailbags as quickly as possible, a duffle coat-wearing trainspotter notes Southern Region No. 33114 at Leamington Spa working 1M02, the 0835 Poole to Liverpool Lime Street. 22 February 1979.

I'm guessing there's a Skoda garage in the arches as No. 47144 soars over five examples while working 1M13, the 11.50 Paddington to Birmingham New Street service, seen here at Leamington Spa. 18 April 1979.

On the bottleneck single line between Leamington Spa and Coventry, No. 47107 has just passed through the then closed Kenilworth station with 4S59, the 11.08 Southampton to Coatbridge Freightliner service. 19 August 1980.

We return to London and start our journey along the West London line

Crossing the Thames on the Cremorne bridge, No. 33016 heads a troop train from Andover to Great Yarmouth. How far the Crompton worked the train is unknown. The four chimneys in the background belong to Fulham Power Station, decommissioned in 1978 and partly demolished in the 1980s. 10 July 1977. (S. Creer)

No. 33024 propels an inspection saloon along the West London line, approaching Earl's Court, which has now been demolished. 5 December 1983. (G. Edwards)

Passing the London Underground Lille Bridge Depot, Gloucester cross-country DMU set L578 is working a Clapham Junction to Kensington Olympia shuttle service.

No. 37044 passes Kensington South Main Signal Box with a Class 302 EMU that is being returned to the Eastern Region after overhaul at Eastleigh Works. June 1983.

Nos 25269 and 25254 are captured running light engine at Kensington Olympia. Interestingly, they were also noted working a Berkhamsted to Scarborough excursion on this day. 13 July 1980.

Passing under Kensington High Street on 4 February 1977, No. 1048 *Western Lady* works a Norwood Junction to Acton freight. A pair of brake tenders can be seen behind the locomotive. The big office block is Charles House, which housed various parts of the Post Office and reportedly also certain secret government departments. The loco had a little over three weeks left in traffic as it was withdrawn on 28 February 1977.

A lonely-looking Kensington Olympia. You can't quite make out the last digit of Class 2505? as it trundles northwards with an overlong load of rails. The barrier wagons either side look like former Conflats. Three members of staff watch the proceedings from the brake van as a trainspotter looks on, *c.* 1977.

Class 31 No. 5511 (later No. 31011) trundles through Kensington Olympia with an inter-regional freight bound for Stratford. The station had an interesting mix of GWR and LMS signals. 30 March 1974. (C. Parker)

Stratford-based No. 47155 runs through the centre road at Kensington Olympia with a short train of 100-ton tank wagons, *c.* 1978.

1979 saw the start of a pair of cross-country services between Manchester Piccadilly and Brighton. Passing through Kensington Olympia *c.* 1979 we find No. 47536 with 1074, the 07.44 train from Manchester to Brighton. It would be 1986 before any of the services would be booked to stop here.

Seen running light engine back to the Southern Region at Kensington Olympia is No. 33056 *The Burma Star*. This was the day of a Railfreight exhibition in the station: 7 March 1981. (A. Gibbs)

Departing from Kensington Olympia with 1S55, the 12.00 SuO Motorail service to Perth, are Nos 25243 and 25254. The locomotives will work the train only as far as Mitre Bridge, Willesden, where an AC electric loco will take over the train for the bulk of the journey north. 31 May 1981.

At White City on the West London line, Nos 33037 and 33057 double-head a heavy Dover to Bescot Speedlink service. The train consists of traffic from the train ferry. 12 April 1982.

With less than half a dozen cars on board, No. 50046 *Ajax* makes light work of this long train forming 1V34, the 07.45 SuO Kensington Olympia to St Austell Motorail service. The train is captured at White City, not long before Motorail services from Olympia ended. 24 May 1981.

An unidentified Class 47/4 has charge of 1M50, the 08.50 Brighton to Manchester Piccadilly service, seen here approaching North Pole Signal Box. The train will then drop down on to the Great Western Main Line at Old Oak Common before heading west to Reading, its next station stop just under two hours after leaving Brighton. September 1985.

At Old Oak Common, the West London line crosses the Great Western Main Line out of Paddington. Here we find Crompton No. 33034 with an engineers' train, illuminated by the low evening sun. 1980. (A. Gibbs)

The 1986 summer timetable saw a big increase in InterCity passenger services over the West London Line, with the previous year's three train pairs a day increased to seven pairs linking Brighton, Dover and Newhaven with the Midlands and North West. No. 47447 is seen here crossing the Paddington branch of the Grand Union Canal with 1M50, the 10.15 Brighton to Manchester Piccadilly. May 1986.

Mitre Bridge, West London Junction, Willesden, and a pair of Class 87s wait to be detached from their Freightliner service. It was here that trains to and from the Southern Region exchanged motive power from an AC electric to a diesel. A Ford D series breakdown truck scuttles across the scrap yard level crossing. July 1983.

For a few years on summer Saturdays the InterCity services to and from Brighton ran to Eastbourne. At West London Junction, Willesden, No. 87022 *Cock o' the North* leads 1M50, the 13.55 SO Eastbourne to Manchester Piccadilly, onto the West Coast Main Line. Next stop is Milton Keynes. 27 May 1989.

Stratford-allocated former Class 48 No. 47114 (D1702) is on the North London line with a short train of Mk 1 GUV parcel vans in tow. The location is Willesden Junction High Level. 30 July 1981.

Willesden Junction High Level and Nos 31108 and 31148 run light engine southwards. 30 July 1981.

Passing through Camden Road station is an unidentified Class 85 with a freight train, which includes a pair of Manchester Pullman coaches in the formation.

The run-down Broad Street station was the terminus of the North London line until its closure in 1986. At one point the station boasted nine platforms. A Class 501 EMU waits to depart on a peak hour service to Watford Junction. April 1973.

Back to Euston station and we find No. 25284 being used to shunt a defective coach. (D. Burton)

A now vanished scene from Britain's railways as No. 85032 sits at Euston with a parcels train. 7 April 1984.

An unidentified Class 25 is captured at South Kenton with an overhead line maintenance train. 29 July 1973. (C. Parker)

With major building work going on at Watford Junction station we find a pair of Class 501 EMUs awaiting their next service. Summer 1984.

No. 86240 *Bishop Eric Treacy* pauses at Watford Junction with what is thought to be 1066, the 08.22 Wolverhampton to Brighton service. From the May 1986 timetable all bar one of the services to the south coast from the Midlands and North West ran via the West Coast Main Line. Full details can be found at my website: www.1S76.com. 17 August 1986.

No. 86402 is found in charge of an unidentified Up InterCity service at Watford Junction. 1986.

No. 86260 *Driver Wallace Oakes G. C.* pauses at Watford Junction with a northbound InterCity service. 17 August 1986.

To allow the Class 501s to be withdrawn, underutilised Class 313s from the Great Northern network were drafted in. No. 313001 in NSE livery can be seen with No. 313010 at Watford Junction. Both these units, renumbered as No. 313201 and No. 313210 respectively, now work on the Coastway services out of Brighton. 17 August 1986.

Departing Wolverton with a stopping service for London is No. 310046. These units were the mainstay of the West Coast Main Line for stopping services between the capital and Birmingham via Northampton from 1963 to 1987.

No. 85038 is captured at Northampton with a long freight train, which includes ferry traffic and flat wagons loaded with Leyland truck cabs. 1 October 1982.

Class 310 No. 310089 waits to depart from Rugby with a stopping service to London Euston via Northampton. The old station was much more atmospheric than the current edifice, even in its run-down state. 16 June 1985.

Stabled in one of the south-facing bay platforms at Rugby is Glasgow Shields Road-allocated No. 81015. 1977. (A. Gibbs)

The photographer was up early to capture this busy scene taken at Coventry at 6.35 a.m. No. 85026 waits to depart with a Down InterCity service, No. 47061 heads south with a Freightliner service and another passenger train leaves for the south. 19 May 1978.

No. 45105 departs from Coventry with 1023, the 15.23 Liverpool Lime Street to Poole cross-country service. Some services changed locomotives here instead of at the more usual Birmingham New Street. 27 May 1981.

Three Spires Junction yard and No. 25311 shunts various wagons, including a single HAA merry-go-round coal hopper, a van and some HTV coal hoppers. 21 April 1984.

APT set No. 370001 leads a Crewe to Rugby test trip through Nuneaton. 30 July 1980. (J. A. Lower)

In bright sunlight, split-headcode Class 40 No. 40130 rests between duties at Nuneaton. 27 August 1980. (J. A. Lower)

Bristol Bath Road-allocated No. 47075 passes through Nuneaton with a train of 100-ton oil tanks. 4 August 1981. (J. A. Lower)

Class 24s were a dying breed when No. 24023 was photographed here at Nuneaton. This example would last another seven months before being withdrawn. September 1977. (J. A. Lower)

With Spaghetti Junction in the background, No. 31173 powers east with 1E66, the 13.15 Birmingham New Street to Norwich. The train is seen here at Bromford Bridge. 11 July 1981.

Saltley Depot, Birmingham, was one of the easier depots to get to and see the locomotives berthed there. On this date we find classes 25, 40, 45 and 47 including No. 45012, No. 40068 and No. 47451 on shed. 1978. (J. A. Lower)

Duddeston station finds No. 85021 basking in the sunshine with an ECS working. As a Southerner it always confused me why the light fittings here had the station name Vauxhall on them. The station had been called Vauxhall and Duddeston until 1974. 17 August 1982.

Three design classics – OK, maybe only two; we can probably discount the Fiat Strada on the billboard, but maybe not the Reliant! A Reliant Regal 3/25 passes under the InterCity 125 heading into New Street. This scene is taken from Duddeston Mill Road. June 1984. (A. Gibbs)

A track gang works on as No. 31158 passes Small Heath with a train loaded with scrap. 15 November 1982.

Making a fine sight as it powers through Barnt Green station is No. 47538, working 1V86, the 09.58 SO Bradford Exchange to Paignton service. 21 July 1979. (P. Barber)

A poorly No. 46051 complete with 6051 headcode is towed out of Birmingham New Street by an unidentified Class 47, probably to Saltley Depot. At least three images of this exist as I took a photo too. 1976. (J. A. Lower)

No. 37103 makes a change from the usual Class 31s on a Norwich to Birmingham New Street service. 1976. (J. A. Lower)

Briefly in daylight before plunging back into the darkness that is Birmingham New Street station, No. 47547 arrives with 1M50, the 09.20 Brighton to Manchester Piccadilly. 27 March 1982. (J. A. Lower)

There should be no complaints about the heating today as No. 45009 makes plenty of steam at Birmingham New Street. There are plenty of trainspotters about on the platforms, too. 9 April 1982.

In the gloom that is Birmingham New Street we find No. 31280 waiting to depart with a parcels train to Peterborough. 21 December 1982.

Diverted via Aston due to a problem elsewhere, No. 86250 *The Glasgow Herald* is seen with 1A46, the 13.27 Wolverhampton to Euston. A few coaches are appearing in the new executive livery; however, apart from one clean coach in blue/grey livery, the rest are filthy. 26 February 1986.

Curving off the line from Walsall at Bescot are 'Choppers' Nos 20016 and 20073 with a long train of HTV coal hoppers. Summer 1979. (A. Gibbs)

I appear to be starting a trend here with a second Reliant car in a picture, this time a Robin. No. 47505 sits alongside it at Bescot. Behind the loco are some army flat wagons with a load of trailers. 26 September 1978.

Taken at St Vincent Street, where the Stour Valley line disappears under Birmingham, No. 45117 is working the ECS from Oxley carriage sidings to New Street, where this train will form 1E23, the 12.17 FO working to York. 14 October 1983.

Slightly further out of Birmingham at the site of the former Monument Lane station is No. 46014 with the stock to form 1E23, the 12.17 FO Birmingham New Street to York service. Today there is little evidence that a station existed here; even the road bridge has been widened to become the A4540 Ladywood Middleway. 9 September 1983.

Powering north at Stafford with an unidentified InterCity service is No. 86249 *County of Merseyside*. April 1984. (P. Barber)

No. 83015 is captured in the shadows of Crewe station working a Euston to Liverpool Lime Street service. An unidentified Class 304 EMU is in the adjacent platform. 1978. (P. Barber)

Another wet day trainspotting at Crewe – just as well it's the summer! Nos 40096, 08329 and 47498 form a cavalcade. August 1978. (A. Gibbs)

After looking around at the Crewe Works open day, there was still time to get some more photos. An unidentified Class 47 is seen here at Crewe North Junction with many enthusiasts watching. 22 September 1979. (A. Gibbs)

A great night-time shot of No. 86327 at Crewe working 1M64, the 15.00 Brighton to Manchester Piccadilly service, which is about twelve minutes late. 15 February 1983. (B. Watkins)

Waiting to depart Crewe with 1V07, the 19.30 to Cardiff Central, is No. 33039. In later years the Cromptons spread their wings far and wide from their Southern Region base. 23 February 1984. (B. Watkins)

No. 86244 *The Royal British Legion* approaches Crewe with 1V59, the 07.20 Glasgow Central to Plymouth service. 17 May 1988.

Approaching Chester station with a Freightliner train bound for Holyhead is No. 40177. August 1978. (A. Gibbs)

March 1984 saw No. 33113 and Gatwick Express sets Nos 8306 and 8201 along with Mk 1 BCK S21273 visit several cities as a Travel Trade preview exhibition for the May launch of the Gatwick Express. Here the combination can be seen leaving Chester en route to Manchester Victoria. 13 March 1984.

Powering through Mostyn on the estuary of the River Dee, No. 45126 makes a fine sight working 1M26, the 13.00 Scarborough to Bangor service. 29 August 1984.

Heading for Holyhead is No. 45057, captured at Rhyl with a Freightliner service. 25 June 1984.

The 1980s saw the Peaks, displaced from the Midland Main Line, take over many of the extended Trans-Pennine workings. At Rhyl we find No. 45108 working 1E08, the 09.15 Bangor to Scarborough service. 28 April 1984.

At Colwyn Bay we find Class 108 DMU M56498 leading a six-car formation. The destination says Liverpool, but the headcode suggests otherwise. 5 August 1973. (C. Parker)

After catching the SO Nottingham to Llandudno Town service as far as Llandudno Junction, I had a few hours to wait before my parents arrived from Brighton. Time wouldn't be wasted as Whistler No. 40022 *Laconia* arrived with a service for Manchester. August 1978. (A. Gibbs)

No. 40042 approaches Llandudno Junction station with an unidentified westbound service. 28 June 1980.

Departing from Llandudno Junction is No. 47448 with a Holyhead to Euston service. 30 May 1980.

Back in the day, summer Saturdays saw many additional services run to seaside resorts around the country. At Llandudno we find one train recently arrived and disgorging its passengers as No. 40008 waits to depart with 1E82, the 13.53 SO to York and Sheffield. The coaches for Sheffield were detached at Huddersfield. 5 June 1982.

Accelerating away from Holyhead is No. 47482 with an unidentified service. 14 June 1979.

Paired up at Holyhead are Nos 47525 and 47511. In the background is the Freightliner terminal; another Class 47 along with a Class 08 can also be seen. 16 August 1989.

With plenty of steam, No. 45067 makes for an atmospheric image at Liverpool Lime Street. The train is forming 1E10, the 15.10 departure to Newcastle. 24 January 1975. (B. Watkins)

The fitters are trying to sort out a problem with the centre cab door and emergency ladder on No. 508041 at Southport. No. 507022 sits alongside. The Class 508s were transferred north from the Waterloo suburban network during 1982. October 1983. (A. Gibbs)

A very grubby No. 150123 arrives at Cheadle Hume station with a service to Crewe. 2 March 1986.

Captured at Alsager, No. 47616 with its enormous *Y Ddraig Goch/The Red Dragon* nameplates works 1D32, the 08.20 Stoke-on-Trent to Llandudno. 4 August 1986. (G. Edwards)

Nos 40028 and 86213 rest at Manchester Piccadilly while the crew of the Class 40 have a discussion. 15 June 1980. (B. Watkins)

I had three trips to Guide Bridge while the Woodhead Route was still in operation, all marred by rain and lots of it on every occasion, apart from this time. Here, No. 40024 approaches Guide Bridge with a short unfitted freight. My Class 76 shots were not good enough to include in the book. August 1978. (A. Gibbs)

No. 37245 runs light engine into Guide Bridge after having just been detached from a train in the yard. August 1978. (A. Gibbs)

Nos 76022 and 76013 are about to pass Hadfield station with an MGR coal train. The Woodhead Route had a little over a year left before closure. 23 June 1980. (S. Clark)

Passing through Romiley station is Peak No. 45022 *Lytham St Annes* working 1E87, the 15.15 Manchester Piccadilly to Harwich Parkeston Quay. This was more often than not my train back to my relatives in Nottingham if I'd been trainspotting in the Manchester area. A former Mk 1 Pullman forms the first class accommodation. 5 July 1979. (B. Watkins)

At Rose Hill Marple we find a Class 104 DMU waiting to depart back to Manchester. 29 May 1978.

A Lincoln-allocated two-car Class 114 DMU formed of vehicles Nos 53002 and 54013 arrives at New Mills Central station. 29 May 1985.

Powering out of the south end of New Mills Tunnel is No. 47532 with 1E87, the 'European', the 11.15 Glasgow Central to Harwich Parkeston Quay. This train effectively replaced the Manchester Piccadilly to Harwich boat train and the Glasgow to Nottingham direct services, but running via Preston and Manchester Victoria rather than the Settle & Carlisle line. 12 September 1985.

In the Derbyshire Peak District at Buxworth, near Chinley, No. 47531 heads east with what is believed to be 1M70, the 10.09 Barrow to Nottingham service. July 1984. (P. Barber)

At Hazel Grove we find Class 108 DMU cars M52062 and M51947 sandwiching Class 104 M59155. The combination is working a Buxton to Manchester Piccadilly service. 14 December 1985.

Choppers Nos 20163 and 20134 are working a long train of ICI limestone hoppers. The train is captured near Disley Tunnel. 2 July 1985.

Some former Class 127 vehicles withdrawn from St Pancras to Bedford duties were converted for parcels and mail services in 1985. At Manchester Victoria we find M55984 and M55974 (formerly M51639 and M51642). 15 December 1985.

A crew change at Manchester Victoria as No. 47306 arrives with an unidentified excursion train. 27 September 1981. (B. Watkins)

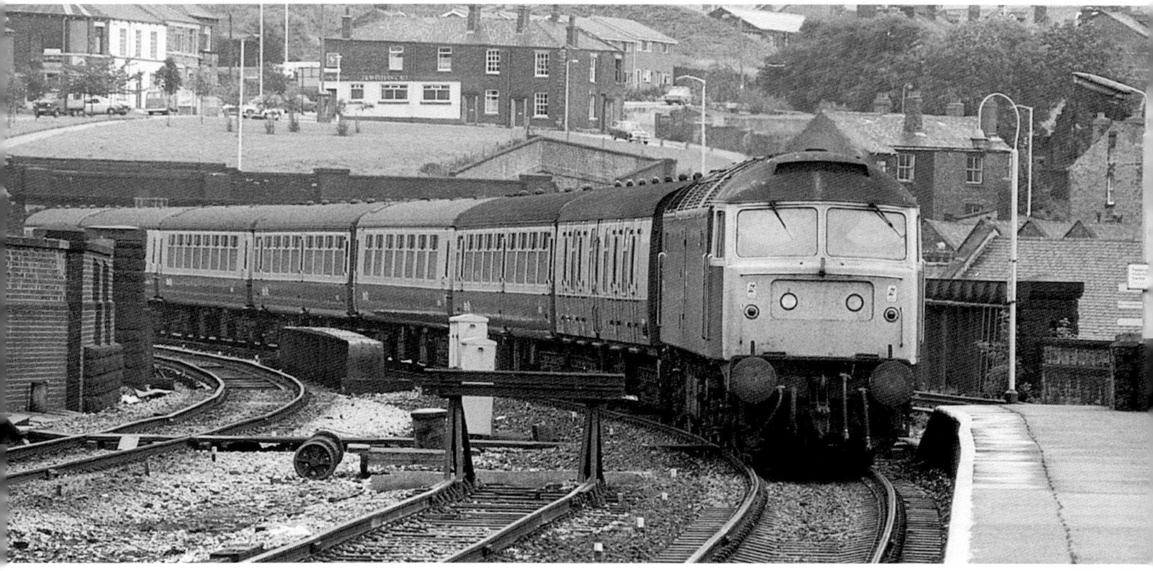

No-heat No. 47365 runs into Stalybridge with a Scarborough to Liverpool Lime Street service. 23 August 1982. (B. Watkins)

No. 86257 powers south at Acton Grange Junction with 1M69, the 09.55 Perth to Kensington Olympia Motorail service. It has a good load of cars on this day. 29 June 1977. (B. Watkins)

A bright sunny day sees No. 47339 heading south with an MGR train at Winwick. 13 April 1981. (B. Watkins)

No. 47454 approaches Preston station with 6Z70, a Class 6 freight train (at least 20 per cent vacuum brake-fitted). A member of the train crew leans out of the rear cab door. 1974.

No. 85019 runs into Preston station with an unidentified southbound service. March 1978.

Ripe for a caption competition, several young trainspotters take notes while the driver of No. 87003 *Patriot* looks back down the train at Lancaster station. 1979.

No. 85022 pauses at Lancaster with an unidentified Down InterCity service. A Metro-Cammell Class 111 DMU can be seen in the adjacent platform. 4 June 1983.

No. 85005 has failed at Lancaster station with a train of ICI soda ash tanks. 9 July 1983.

No. 40082 starts to lay down some clag as it gets away from Lancaster station with 1F30, the 08.22 Barrow-in-Furness to Liverpool Lime Street service. 5 May 1984.

No. 81009 heads south at Shap with a lightly loaded 1M69, the 11.30 Stirling to Euston Motorail service. There are nearly as many coaches as cars. 10 June 1988. (M. Hull)

We now return to London and the Midland Main Line and its branches from St Pancras to Carlisle

On the stops at St Pancras we find Peak No. 45134 looking rather shabby. It has just been detached from its train. I've always had a soft spot for St Pancras, it being the start of many journeys to my relatives in Nottingham. I never went in The Shires bar … honest!

At St Pancras a crowd gathers around D200 (No. 40122) as it starts up. Its twin plumes of exhaust start to fill the station. It is working the 02.00 parcels train to Derby, having arrived in London earlier the previous evening with a railtour. No. 317345 waits to depart with the 00.45 train to Bedford. 9 September 1984.

A Class 127 DMU is captured at St Albans on a Bedford to St Pancras working. Despite it being 1978, the rear coach, M51593, is still displaying a headcode, not required since January 1976. 24 July 1978.

Syston Junction to the north of Leicester finds No. 47537 in charge of the Up 'Master Cutler'. 7 July 1977.

Down in the long grass the photographer captures No. 45135 heading south with just a Mk 1 coach and SR CCT van in tow. 7 July 1977.

Split-headcode-fitted Peak No. 45027 has a mixed bag of ballast wagons in tow at Loughborough. The Brush Electrical Machines factory, which built many of BR's locomotives, can be seen in the background. 1980.

Class 20s are synonymous with the 'Jolly Fisherman' workings to Skegness. At Loughborough we find No. 20058 and a sister locomotive chirping away while the driver and railman have a conversation. The train appears to have stopped very short in the platform.

The Ratcliffe-on-Soar Power Station cooling towers dwarf No. 25044 and No. 25097 running light engine. 21 September 1981. (J. A. Lower)

Class 25 No. 25134 has charge of a bridge inspection train, checking out the brickwork on the Midland Main Line bridge crossing the River Trent at Trent Lock. April 1980. (J. A. Lower)

No. 47344 powers through Trent Junction with the Birmingham Lawley Street to Beeston Freightliner service. 13 May 1981. (J. A. Lower)

No. 37269 heads south at Stenson Junction with a train of 45-ton TTA tank wagons. The line towards Castle Donnington can be seen in the distance, branching off to the right. 2 August 1979. (J. A. Lower)

Stenson Junction to the south-west of Derby is where the Castle Donnington and Stoke lines join the NE–SW route. Here we find former tablet catcher-fitted No. 25270 leading No. 25056 with an engineers' train. There used to be a pub next to the railway line and canal, which I see is now an Indian restaurant. 30 July 1981. (J. A. Lower)

The Peaks were stalwarts of the NE–SW services, especially the Class 46s. At Burton-on-Trent No. 46014 powers south with an unidentified service. 2 June 1982.

Heading south through Tamworth High Level platforms is No. 45046 with a train of loaded coal hoppers. 25 June 1985.

Curving off the line from Derby, No. 47328 approaches Water Orton with a loaded merry-go-round coal train. June 1978. (J. A. Lower)

In the Railway Technical Centre at Derby is LEV1, the first Leyland National bus-bodied prototype railcar. This was to spawn several more prototypes and Classes 140–142, 155 and a single passenger coach. July 1979. (J. A. Lower)

Peaks pass at Derby. No. 45053 heads south as the guard leans out of window, while No. 46053 arrives with an unidentified cross-country service. 26 February 1977. (B. Watkins)

The driver of No. 47366, still in two-tone green livery, leans out of the cab to talk to the station staff at Derby. 1977. (J. A. Lower)

Approaching Derby in the snow is No. 46047, working an unidentified NE–SW service. 1979. (J. A. Lower)

With a fair coverage of snow, No. 31177 heads north from Derby with a freight train. 1979. (J. A. Lower)

No. 45135 *3rd Carabinier* heads out of Derby with a St Pancras to Sheffield service. June 1979. (A. Gibbs)

No. 25274 is smokin' as it heads north with a train of empty steel plate wagons. June 1979. (A. Gibbs)

Just of north of Derby and heading south, No. 45060 works a SAGA Holidays special from Newcastle to a holiday resort: it could be Torquay, Newquay, Margate, Eastbourne or Portsmouth. June 1979. (A. Gibbs)

A Class 120 Swindon cross-country DMU is captured at Duffield with a Derby to Matlock service. 3 April 1982. (J. A. Lower)

At the site of the closed Coxbench station No. 47198 heads up the branch line with an empty MGR coal train from Willington Power Station to Denby open-cast mine. 29 September 1981. (J. A. Lower)

At Matlock station we find the second of the prototype Metro-Cammell Class 151 DMUs, No. 151002. After only four years in service they were withdrawn and stored for many years at Llandudno Junction. 1985. (A. Gibbs)

A bright winter's day sees No. 25048 head south at Meadow Lane level crossing with an RTC (Railway Technical Centre) train consisting of a BR-built ferry van, former Autocoach Laboratory No. 1 and a VDA van. 11 December 1980. (J. A. Lower)

Meadow Lane level crossing at Trent Junction and No. 25325 works a Freightliner train from Lawley Street, Birmingham, to Beeston. 11 December 1980. (J. A. Lower)

At Toton Yard you could hear the chirping of scores of Class 20s whenever you visited, before even getting out of the car. Here we find Nos 20051 and 20087 working an empty MGR train. 15 April 1988.

At the south end of Toton Yard, No. 44007 will make easy work of this short train. Formerly named *Ingleborough*, the loco was withdrawn at the end of November 1980 and cut up a year later. 1978. (J. A. Lower)

No. 47155 approaches its destination: the Freightliner terminal at Beeston, to the south of Nottingham. The Shipstones maltings have sadly been demolished. 25 June 1985.

No. 47480 *Robin Hood* heads past Wilford Power Station after being named at Nottingham station by the Lord Mayor. 23 November 1979. (A. Gibbs)

Passing through Nottingham station No. 37201 has a train of anhydrous ammonia tank wagons in tow. A barrier wagon separates the loco from the load. In the background on the London Road bridge is a Barton Transport bus. 30 August 1980. (J. A. Lower)

In Nottingham station No. 47444 has just been named *University of Nottingham* by the chancellor of the university. 14 May 1981. (J. A. Lower)

With a Class 150 peeking into view on the left, No. 31464 arrives at Nottingham with 1L82, the 06.50 SO Manchester Piccadilly to Great Yarmouth service. 28 May 1988. (P. Barber)

With the skyline of Nottingham in the background a pair of Class 20s curve through Lenton Junction. The service is unknown, but is possibly the Saturdays-only Skegness to Alfreton and Mansfield Parkway train. August 1977.

One of my favourite photos that my uncle took was this one of Nos 31282 and 31310 reflected in the car door mirror at Ilkeston. The industrial estate next to the railway line was an easy place to park and watch the streams of trains pass by. 8 May 1981. (J. A. Lower)

Taking the line towards Toton and Nottingham, No. 40154 is seen working an engineers' train. 15 June 1980. (A. Gibbs)

Not the expected Peak or Class 47 coming towards us as Deltic No. 55018 *Ballymoss* throbs past. It is working a railtour, 'The White Rose'. Originating at King's Cross, it ran to York and back via Sheffield, incorporating Tinsley depot open day. 15 June 1980. (A. Gibbs)

Tractor No. 37219 heads north at Clay Cross with a train of empty steel coil wagons. 23 July 1980. (J. A. Lower)

The former station site at Clay Cross was a great place to go trainspotting: an overbridge and lineside views without having to even leave the car. No. 47360 powers north with a train of 100-ton tank wagons. 23 July 1980. (J. A. Lower)

Nos 20059 and 20066 are seen northbound at Clay Cross with a freight train. The first load in the train is No. 08729, returning to its home depot of Tinsley after overhaul. 3 March 1981. (J. A. Lower)

With a long train of brand-new Seacow hopper wagons, No. 47265 takes the line towards Derby at Clay Cross. 16 September 1981. (J. A. Lower)

Heading south at Clay Cross, No. 31437 is working 1086, the 14.00 Leeds to Brighton service. This train also conveyed coaches from Hull. The equivalent northbound service originated at London Paddington. The lines to the right curve off towards the Erewash Valley and Nottingham while the Class 31 will head to Derby. 19 April 1986.

Taken from the exchange sidings for the Avenue carbonisation plant at Clay Cross, No. 45041 *Royal Tank Regiment* is seen working a cross-country service as it passes No. 37007 on a train of steel rods. 6 June 1979. (J. A. Lower)

Rush hour at Skipton sees Nos 31405 and 47440 double-head what is probably 1M43, the 10.42 Leeds to Carlisle, while No. 31327 *Phillips-Imperial* and No. 31229 arrive from the Grassington branch with a loaded stone train. 18 September 1987. (M.Hull)

There is not much evidence of the long, hot summer of 1976 yet as Nos 25296 and 25199 trundle along the Grassington branch at Rylstone. The huge quarry is the sole source of traffic on the route. 21 June 1976. (G. Roose)

Working a Leeds to Morecombe service, this three-car Class 111 DMU was captured just north of Skipton at Niffany Bridge. 10 June 1974. (S. Creer)

At Hellifield we find No. 47540 working 1S68, the 10.20 Nottingham to Glasgow Central service. A young lad leans out of the leading droplight on the buffet car for the expected thrash. 13 May 1982. (G. Roose)

On the Copy Pit line near Walk Mill, Burnley, No. 37141 works west with a train of bitumen tank wagons bound for Preston docks. 7 December 1981. (G. Roose)

With threatening skies in the distance we find 'Rat' No. 25248 running light engine near Gisburn on the Blackburn to Hellifield line. 29 March 1982. (G. Roose)

Heading south at Long Preston, No. 40184 makes a fine sight with its mixed freight train.

A mixed bag of wagons can be seen behind No. 47051 at Long Preston, including ICI Mond tanks, a Presflo and several ventilated vans. 23 May 1980. (G. Roose)

Peak No. 45002 is at Settle Junction, where the lines on the left branch off towards Clapham. The loco is working 1M86, the 11.50 Glasgow Central to Nottingham service. 1 May 1982. (G. Roose)

At Horton in Ribblesdale, No. 45063 is captured working 1S68, the 09.41 Leicester to Glasgow Central service. 1 May 1982. (G. Roose)

A super photo with spring daffodils as No. 45053 arrives at Settle. The train is 1M86, the 10.45 Glasgow Central to Nottingham. 15 April 1977. (B. Watkins)

With a northbound fitted freight in tow, No. 40008 approaches Ribblehead Viaduct. 28 July 1980. (A. Coombe)

Dent Head and an unidentified Class 47/4 powers through the Pennines.

On a beautiful autumn day we find No. 47423 crossing Arten Gill Viaduct with 1E20, the 10.40 Carlisle to Leeds service. 15 October 1986. (M. Hull)

At Ais Gill Nos 31208 and 31212 power south with 1E42, the 17.00 Carlisle to Leeds service. 10 July 1988. (M. Hull)

The splendour of the Pennines captured at Garsdale as No. 47649 works 1M09, the 08.42 Leeds to Carlisle service. There is still snow on the distant hills. 18 March 1988. (M. Hull)

Powering through the Pennines with 1S49, the 07.15 Nottingham to Glasgow Central, is No. 40032. The train is caught on camera at Newlands Road between Kirkby Stephen and Appleby. 30 March 1978.

A heavily loaded Motorail service with No. 85021 in charge approaches Carlisle station. A Mk 1 GUV leads the carflats. 11 September 1981.

The shunter detaches No. 47819 from its train at Carlisle; the service is unknown. August 1989.

In bright autumnal sunshine I found myself at Carlisle changing trains en route to Scotland. No. 86205 is berthed on the left and just arrived is No. 86255, seen working 1V95, the 13.35 Glasgow Central to Taunton. 28 October 1980. (A. Gibbs)